This Coloring Book Belongs to

....

Copyrights 2021 Floriated Stress Relieving Decorative Floral Adult coloring book By Zohreh Mohammadi

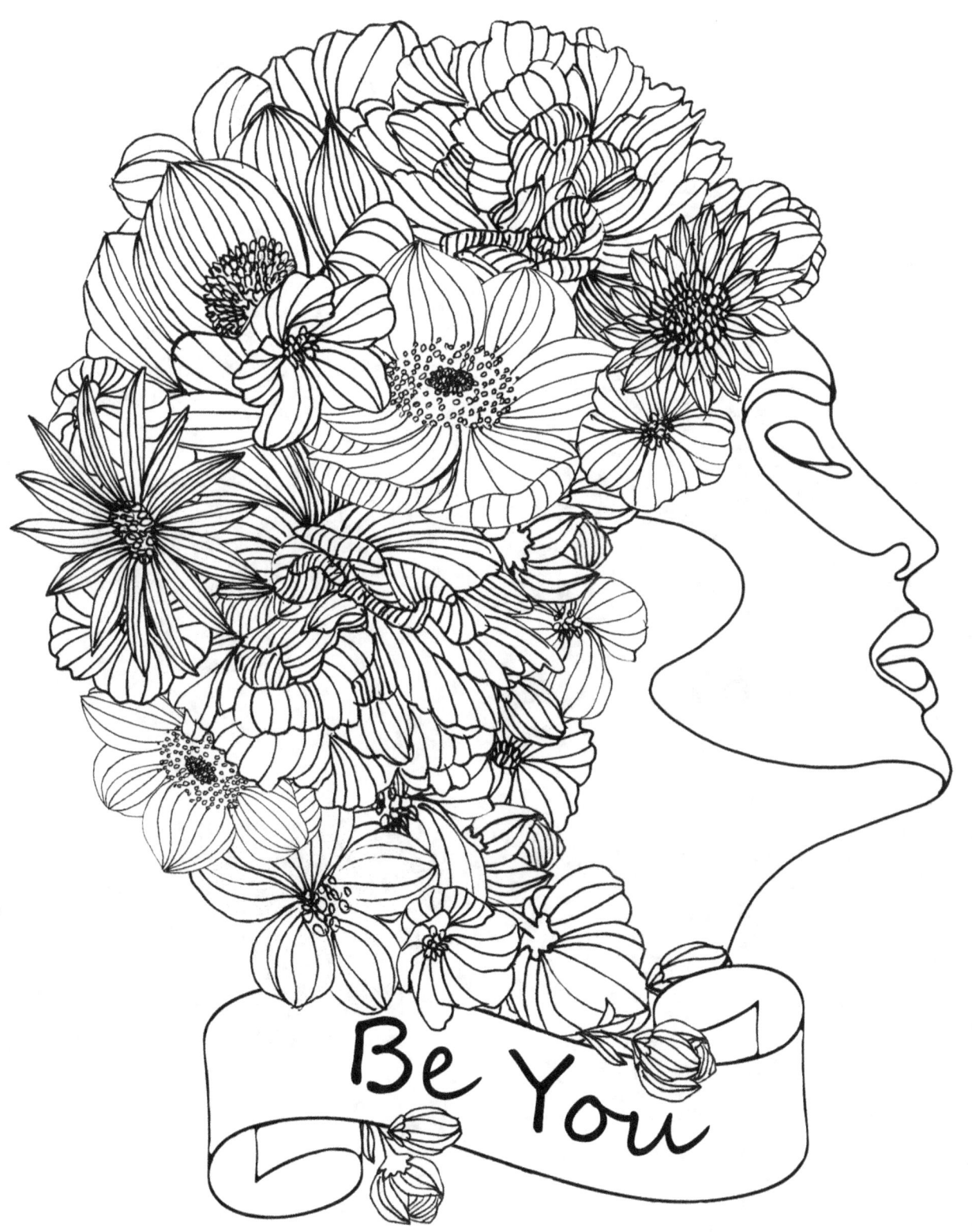

Chrysanthemum bouquet

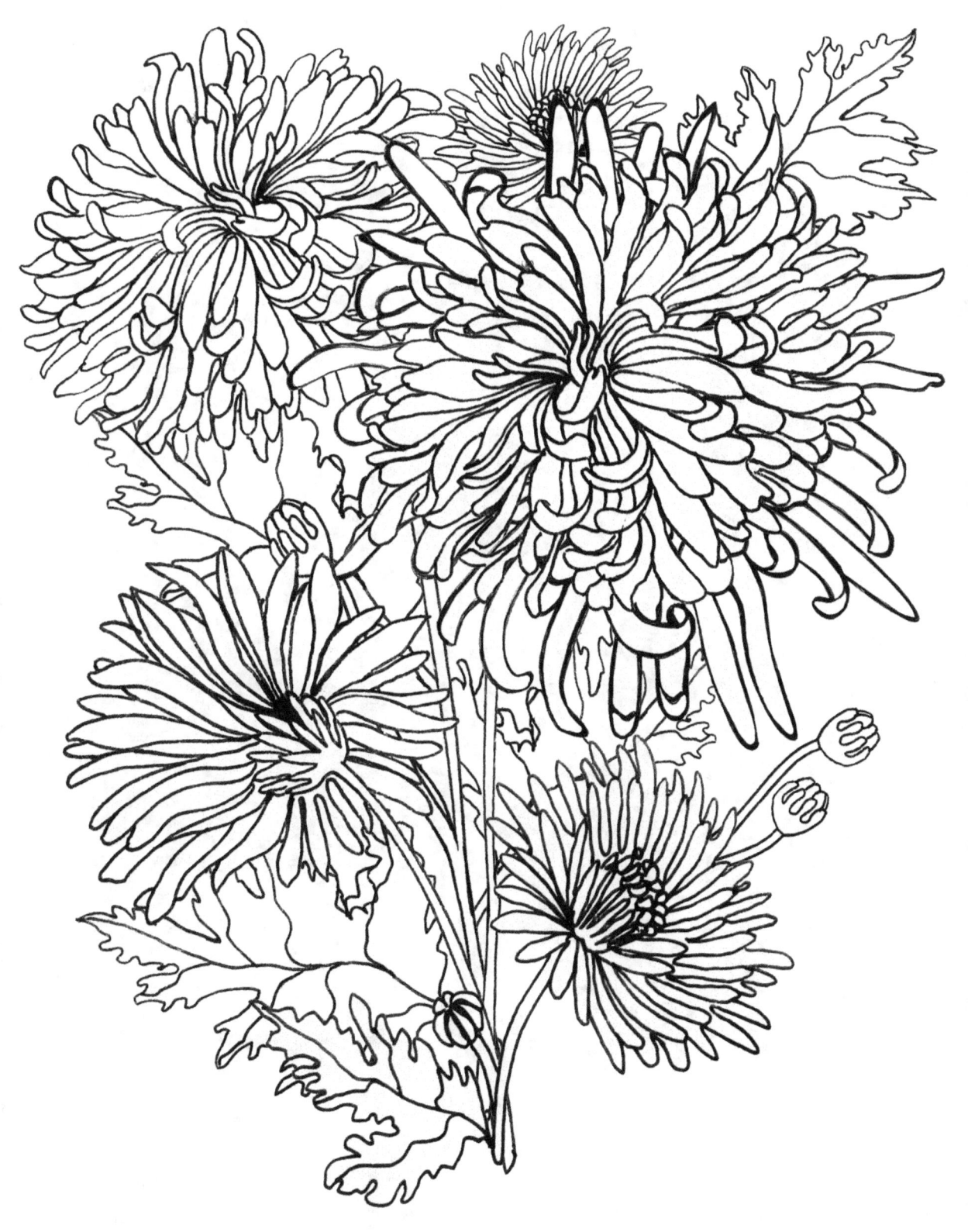

Sparrow and daisies

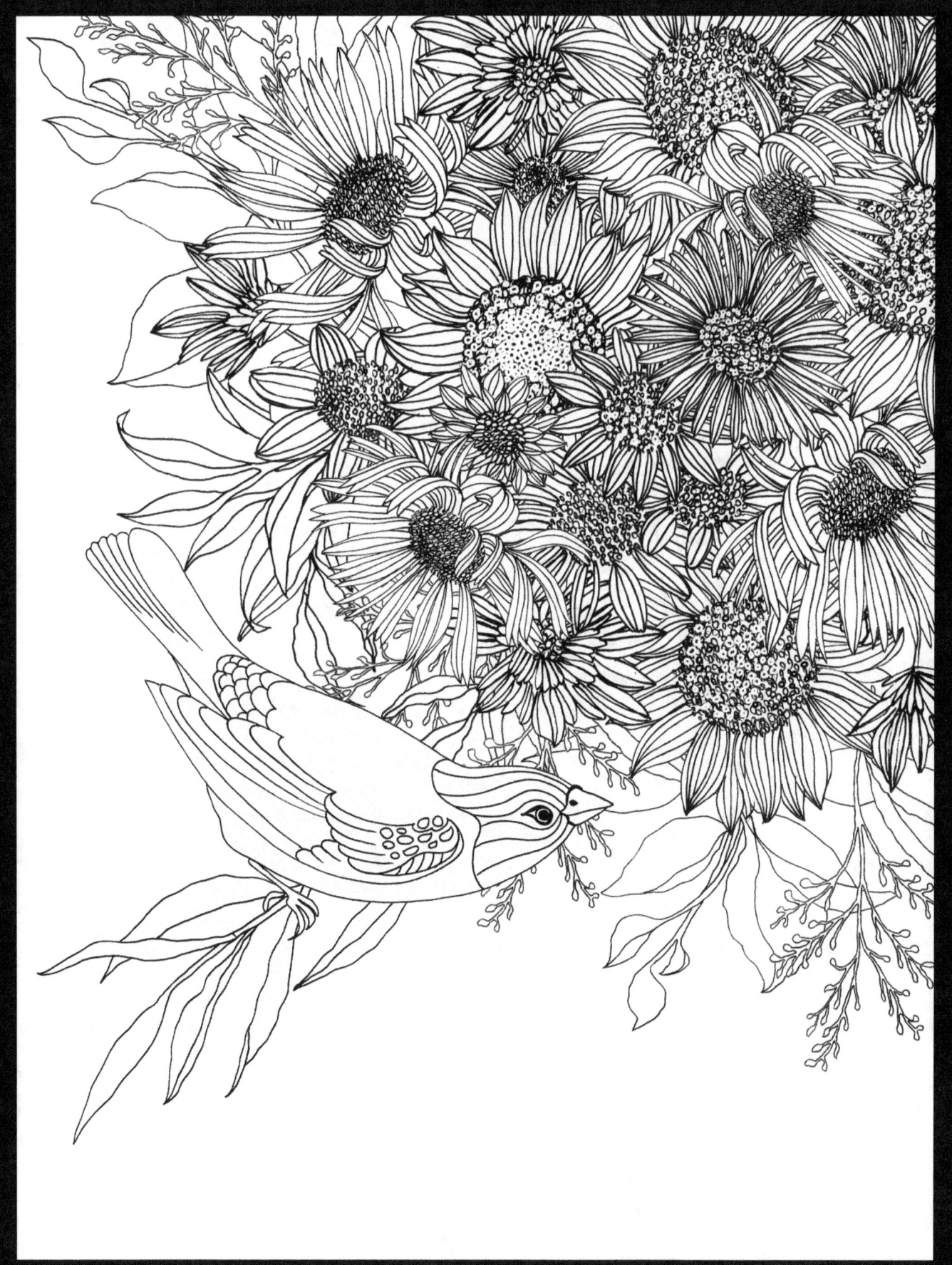

Mandala flower

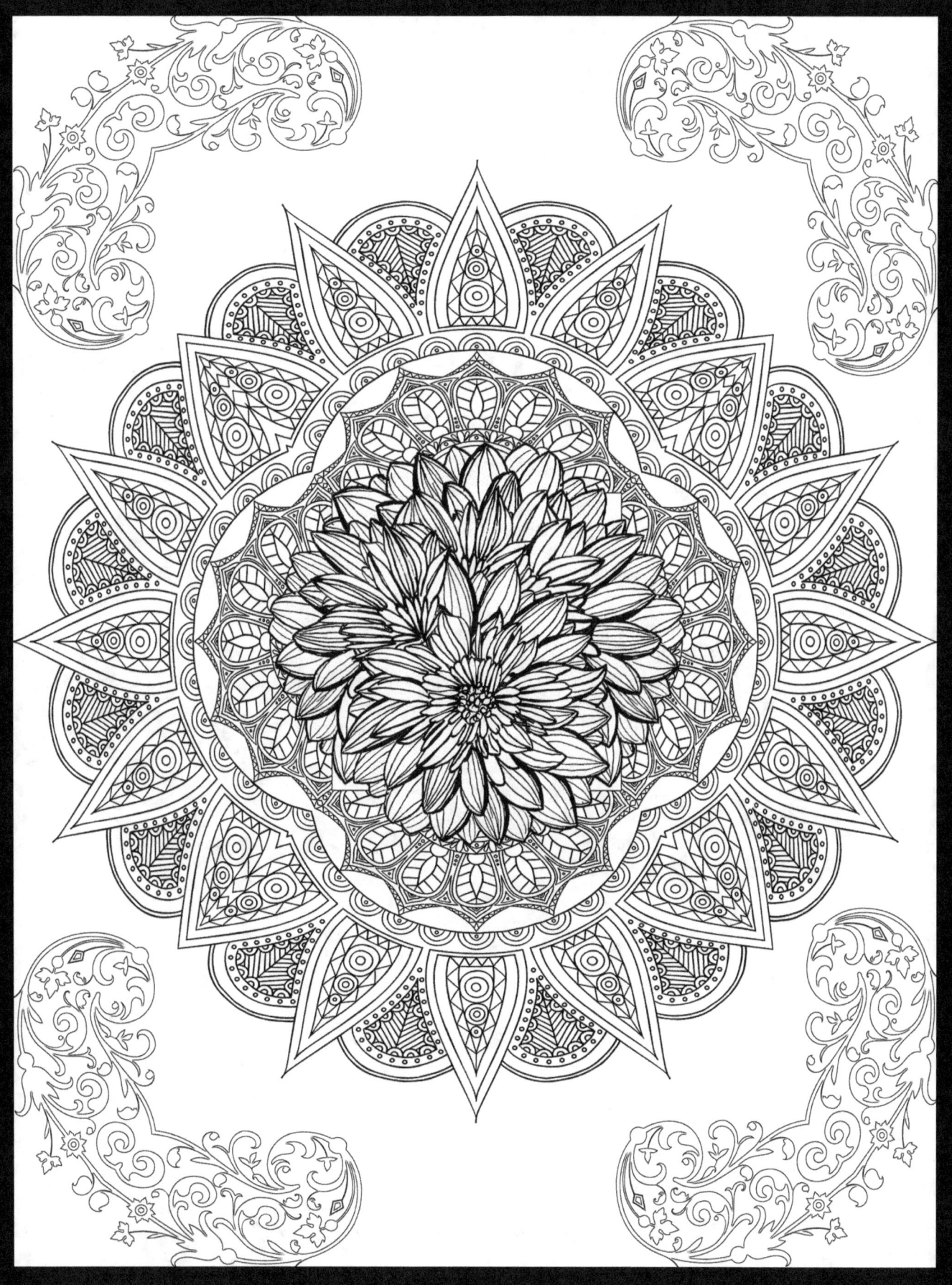

Garden fairy tail

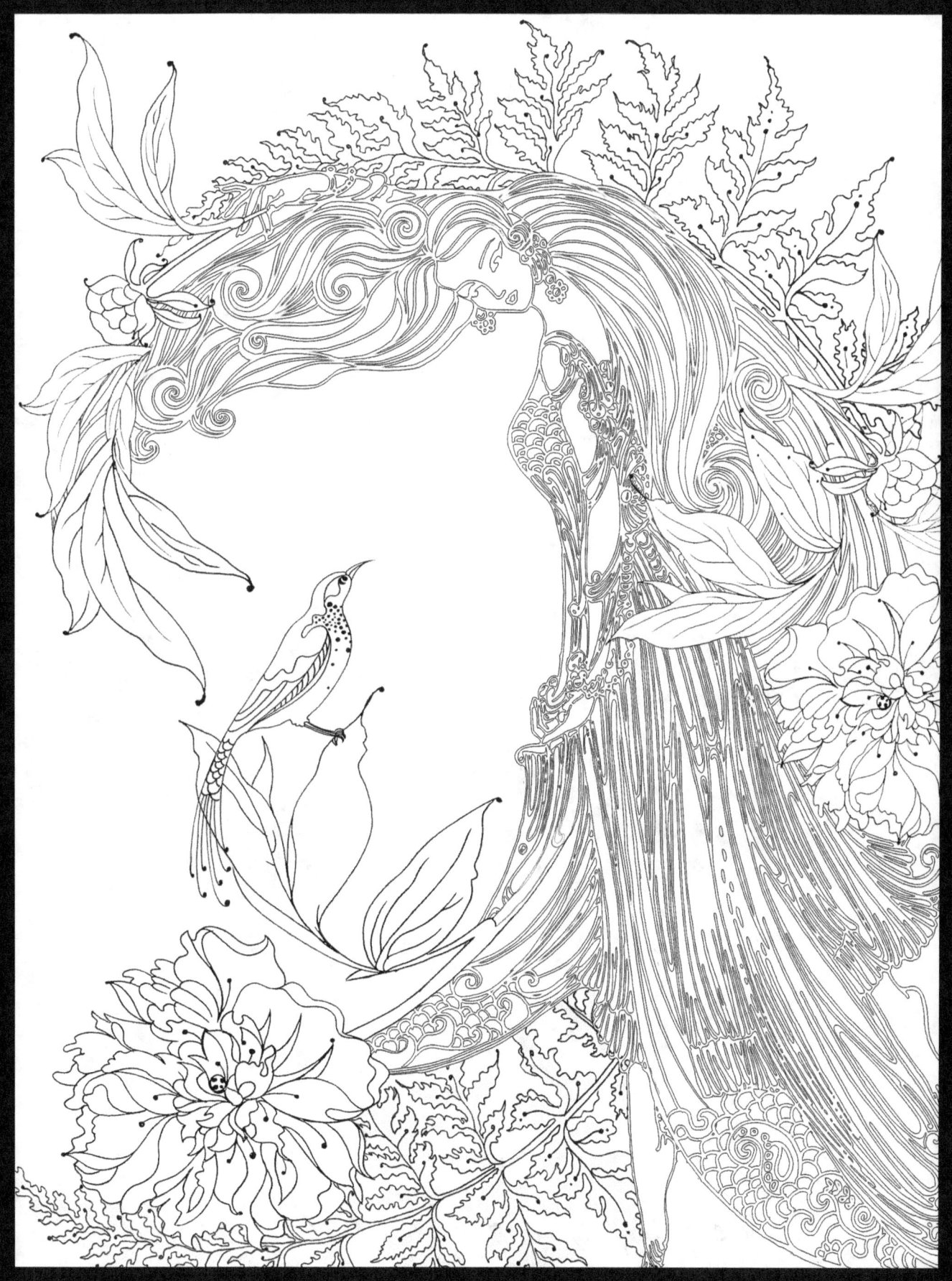

Elegant bouquet of flowers

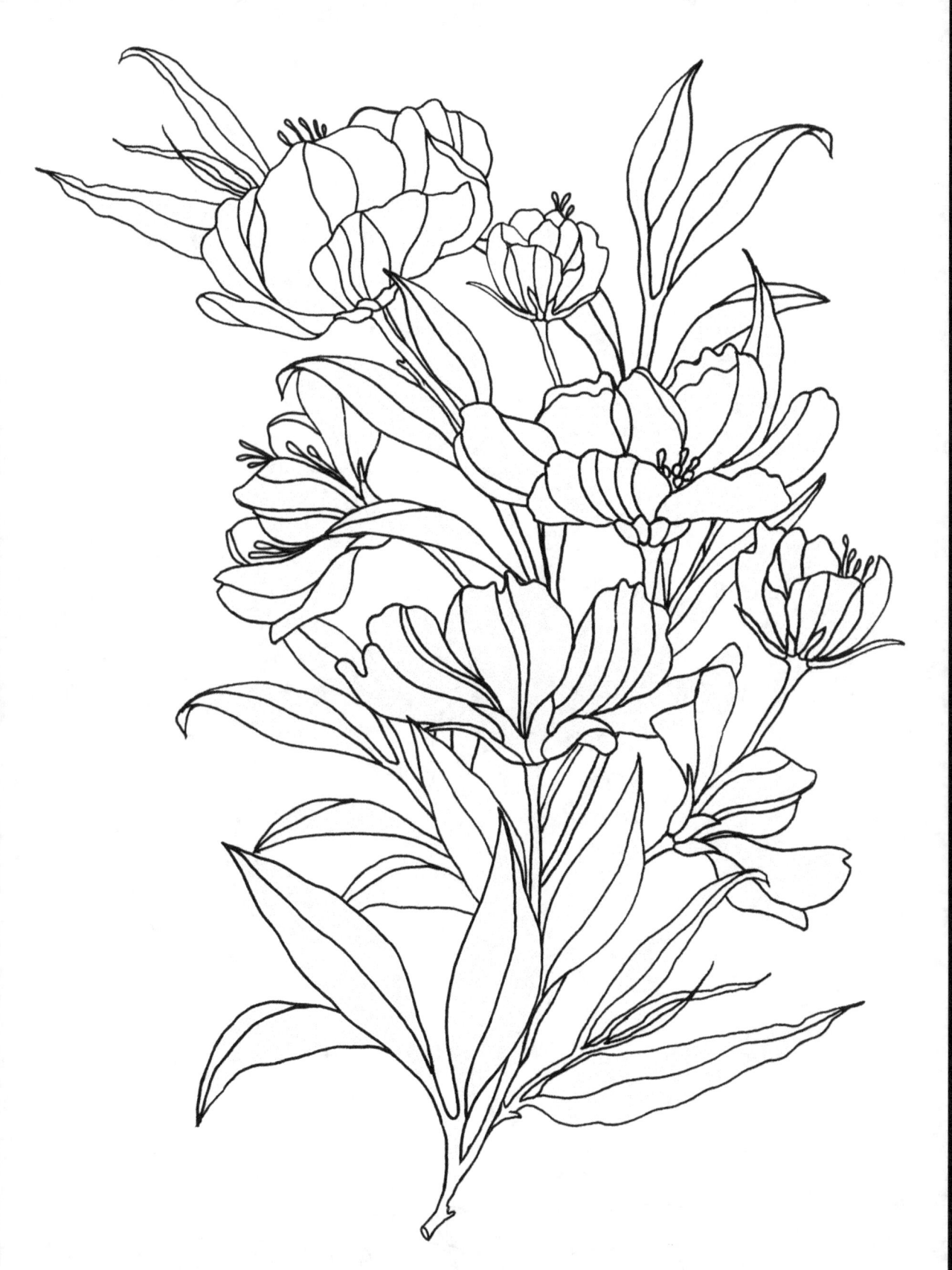

Faces & Flowers

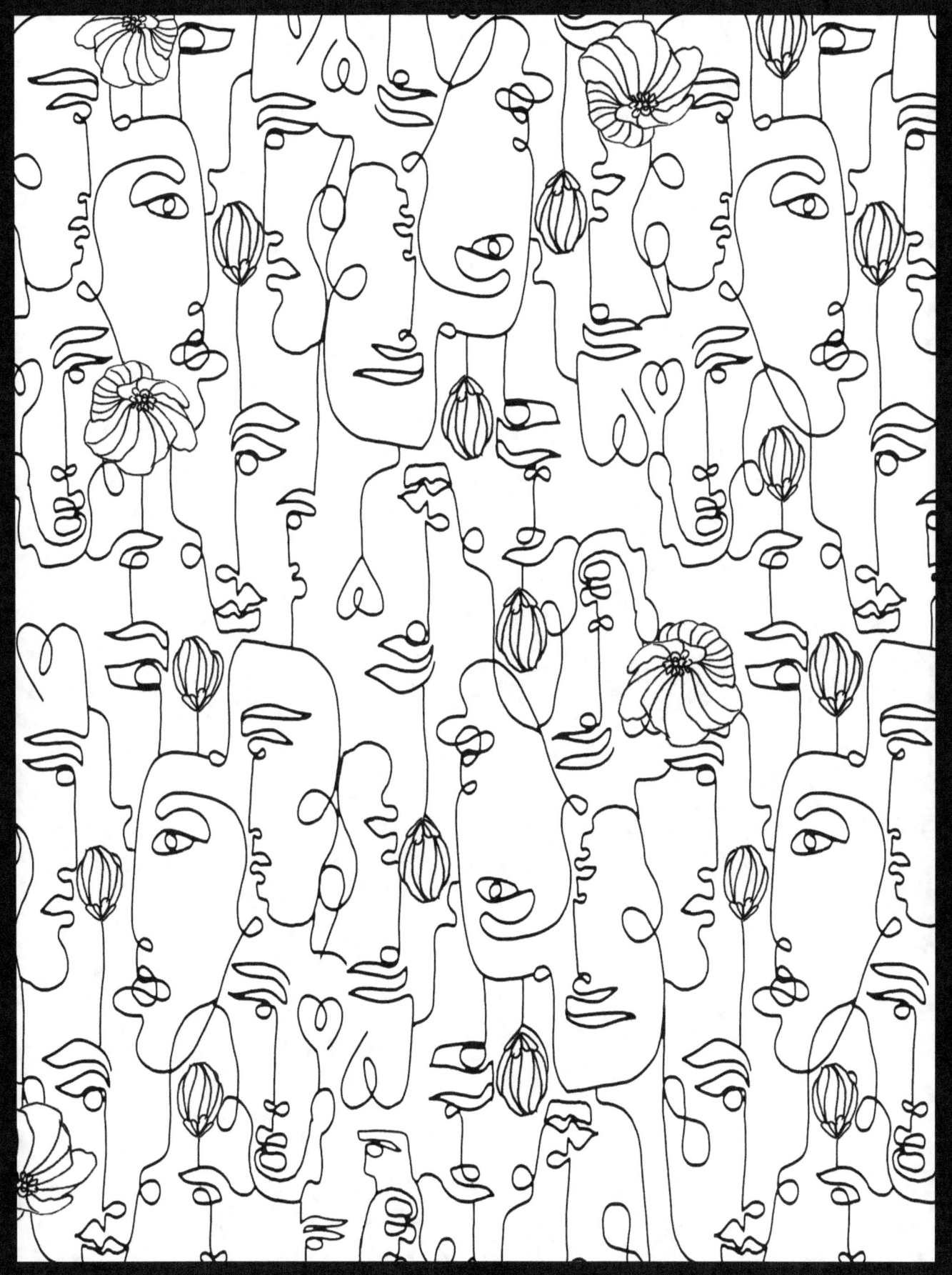

Roses of garden

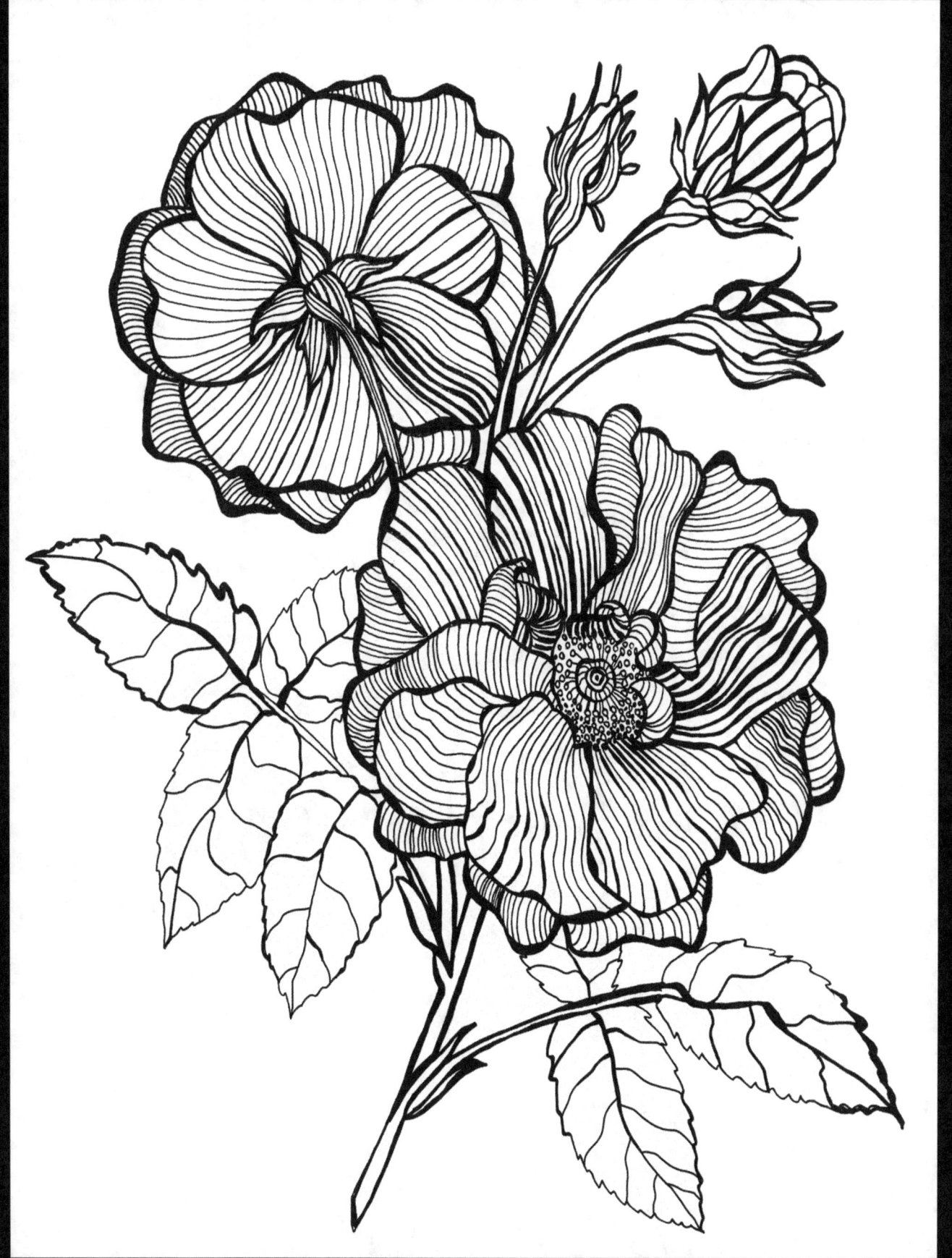

Love laugh live

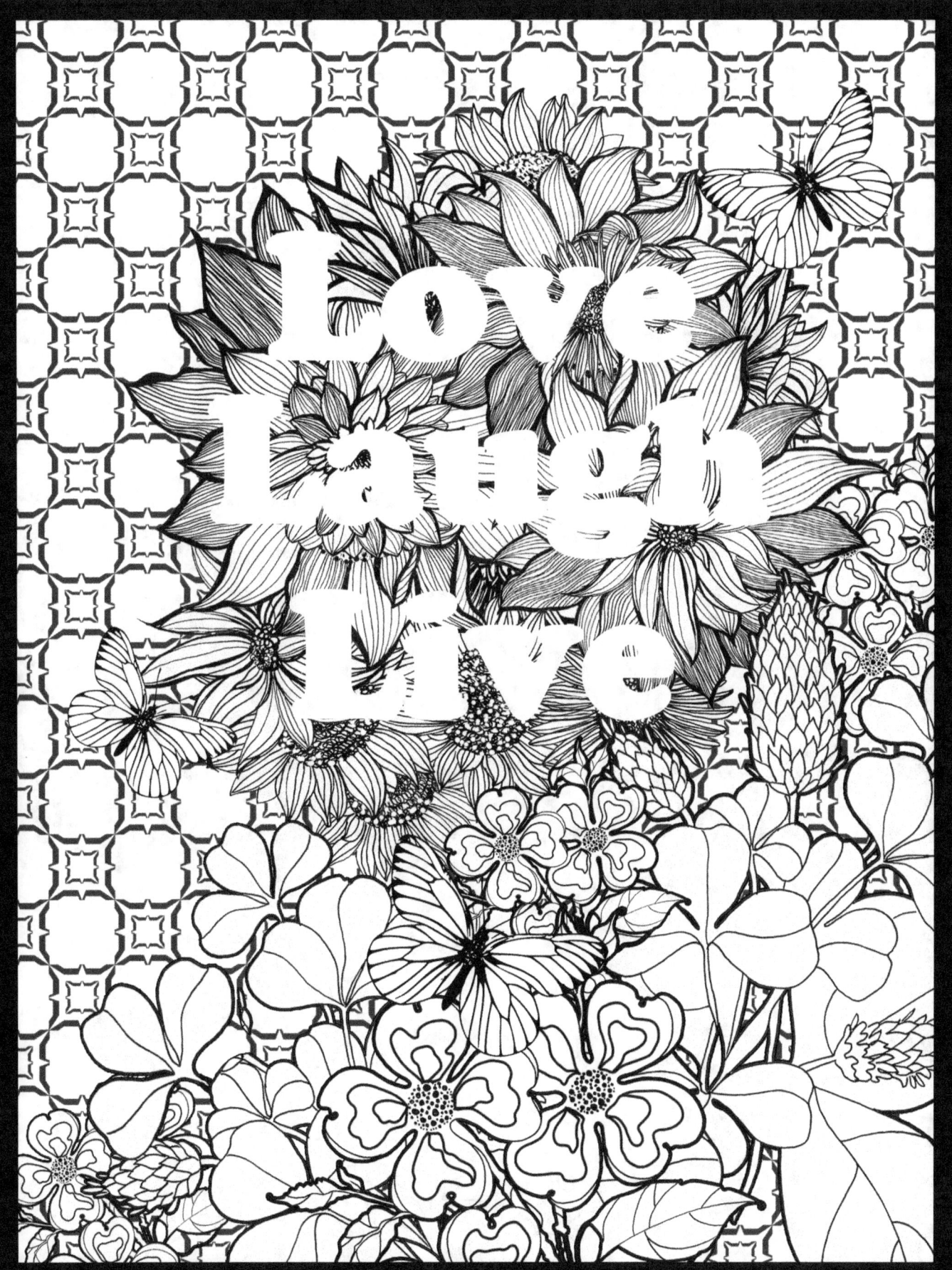

Secret love

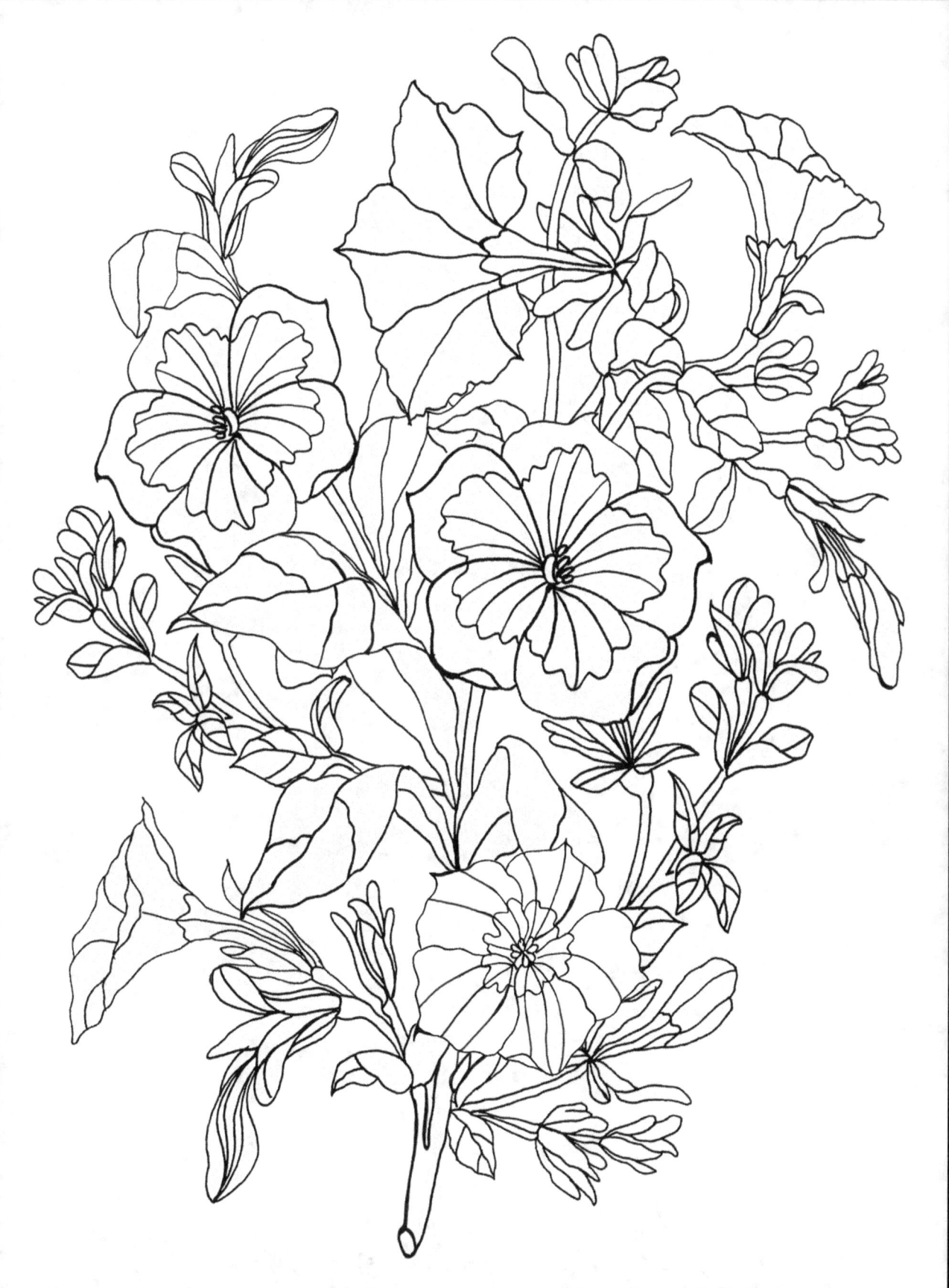

Zen mandala garden

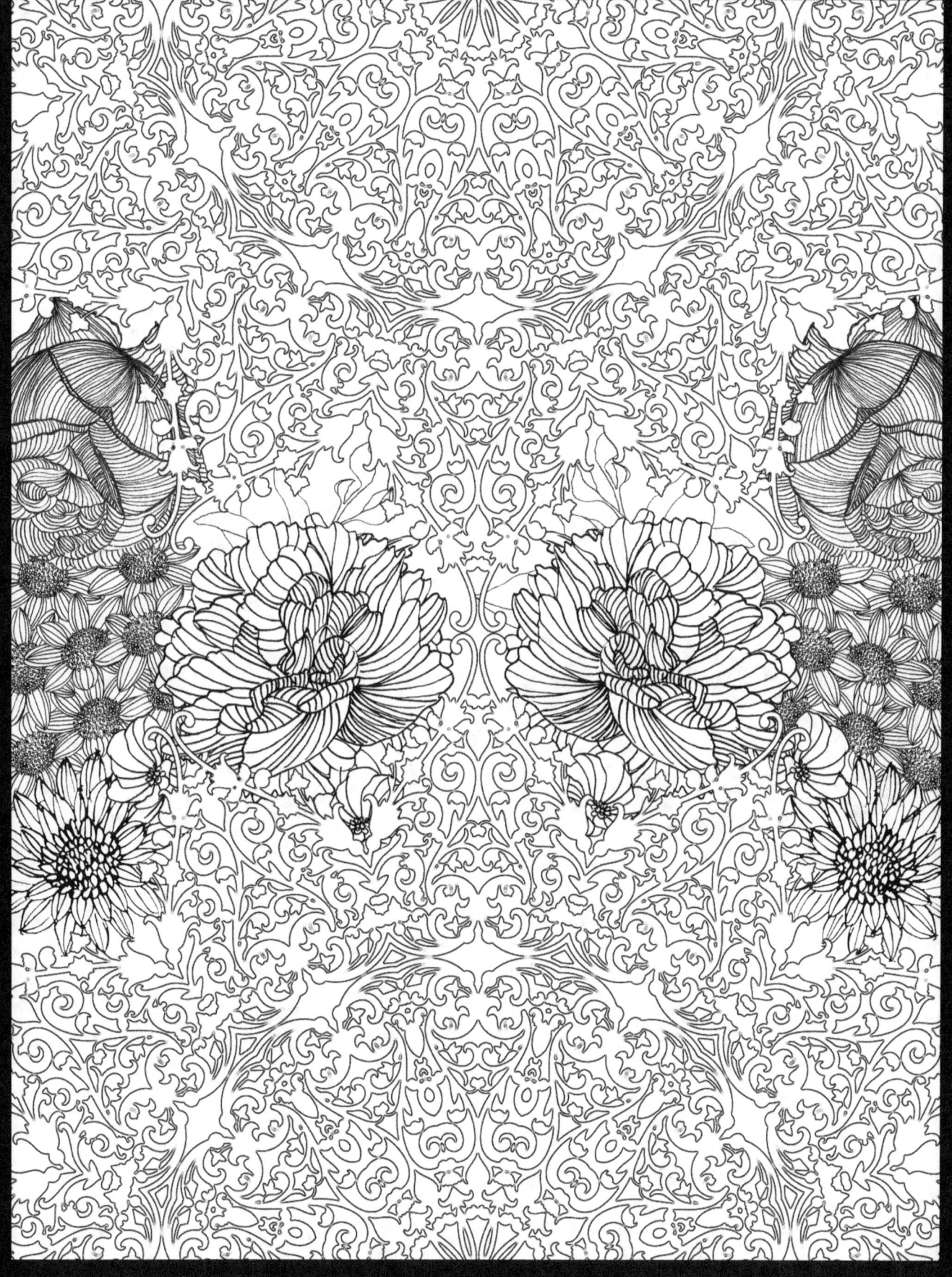

Pumpkin flowers

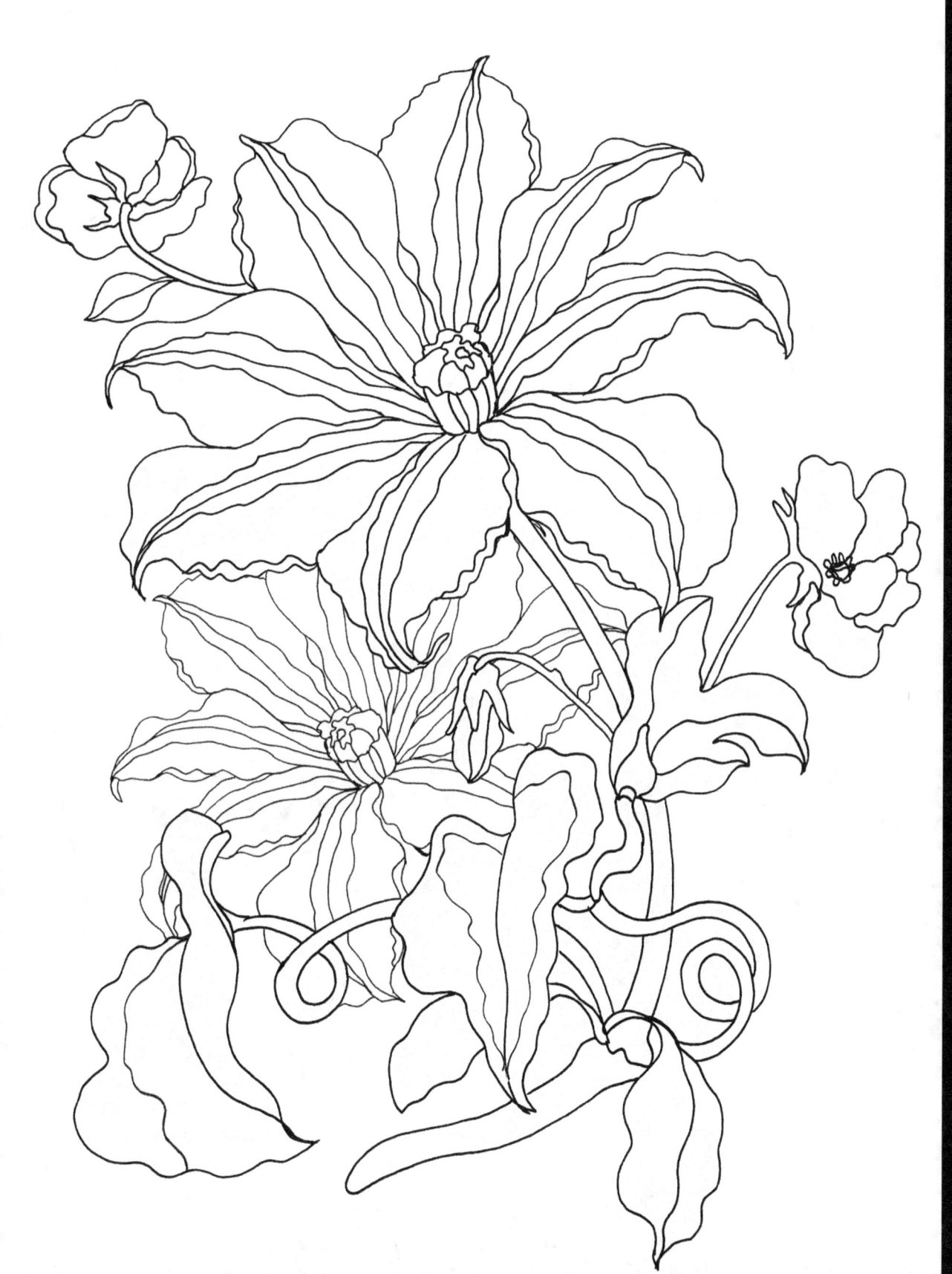

Floral challenge

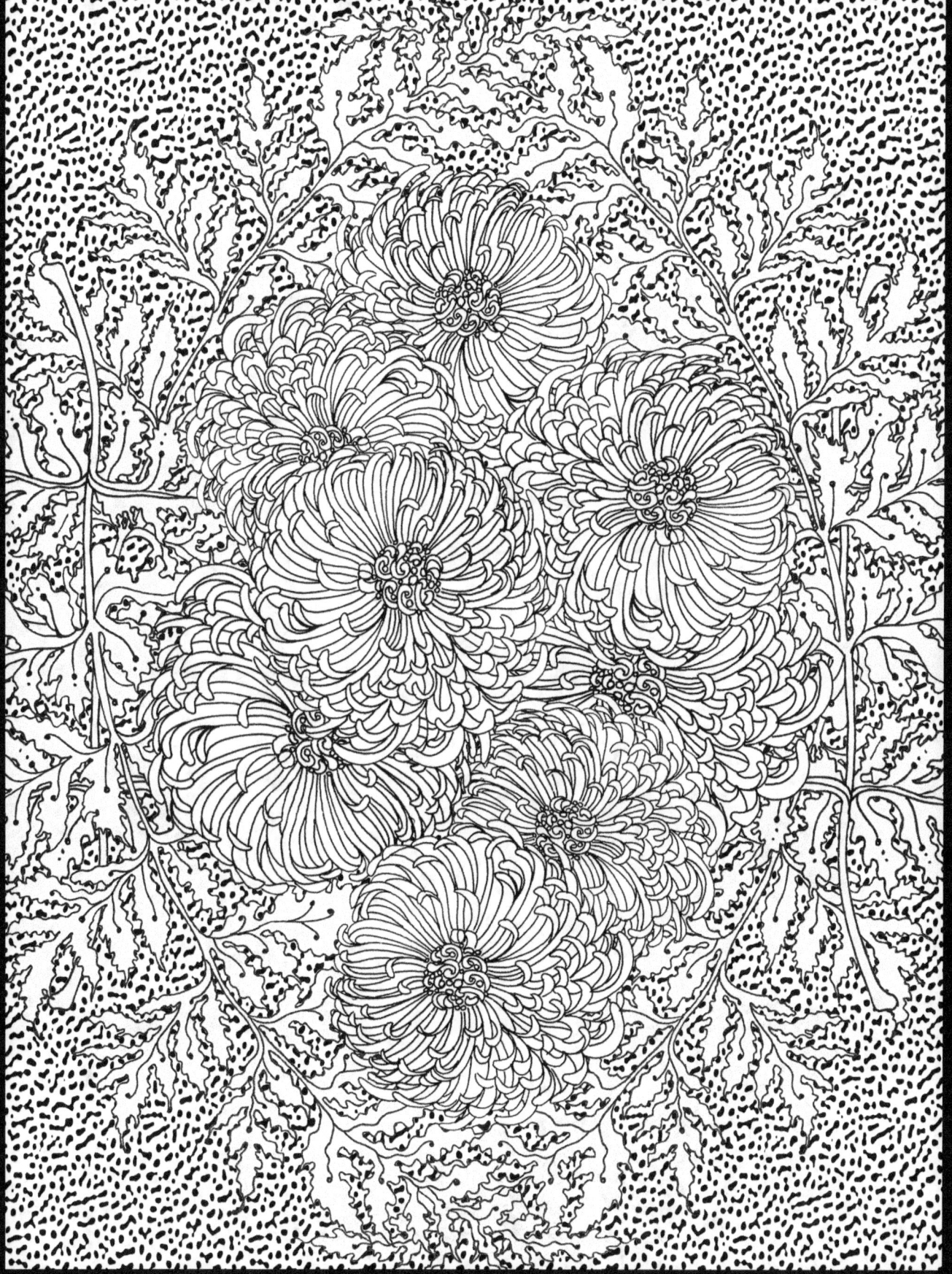

Monstera mania

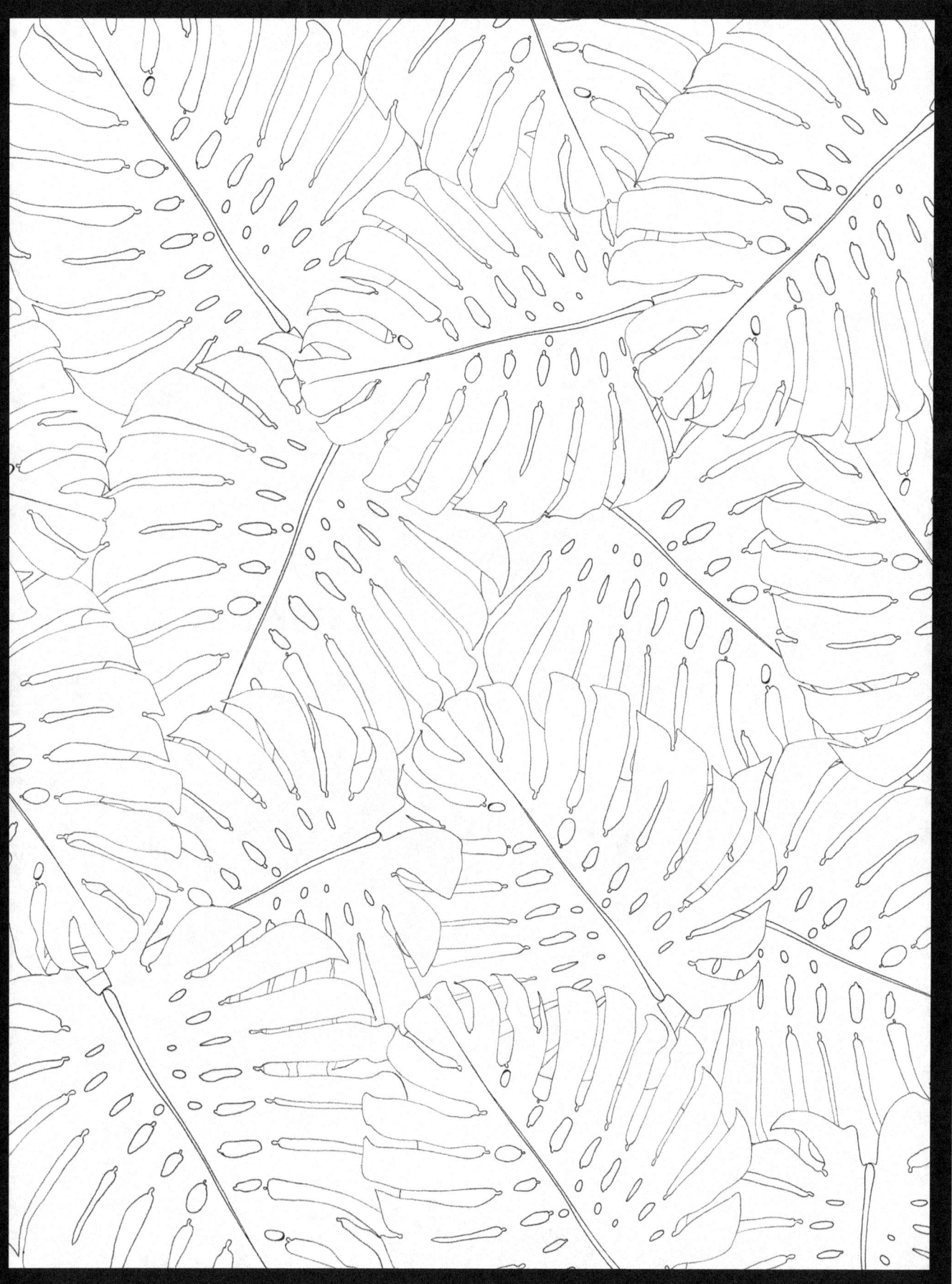

Love letter

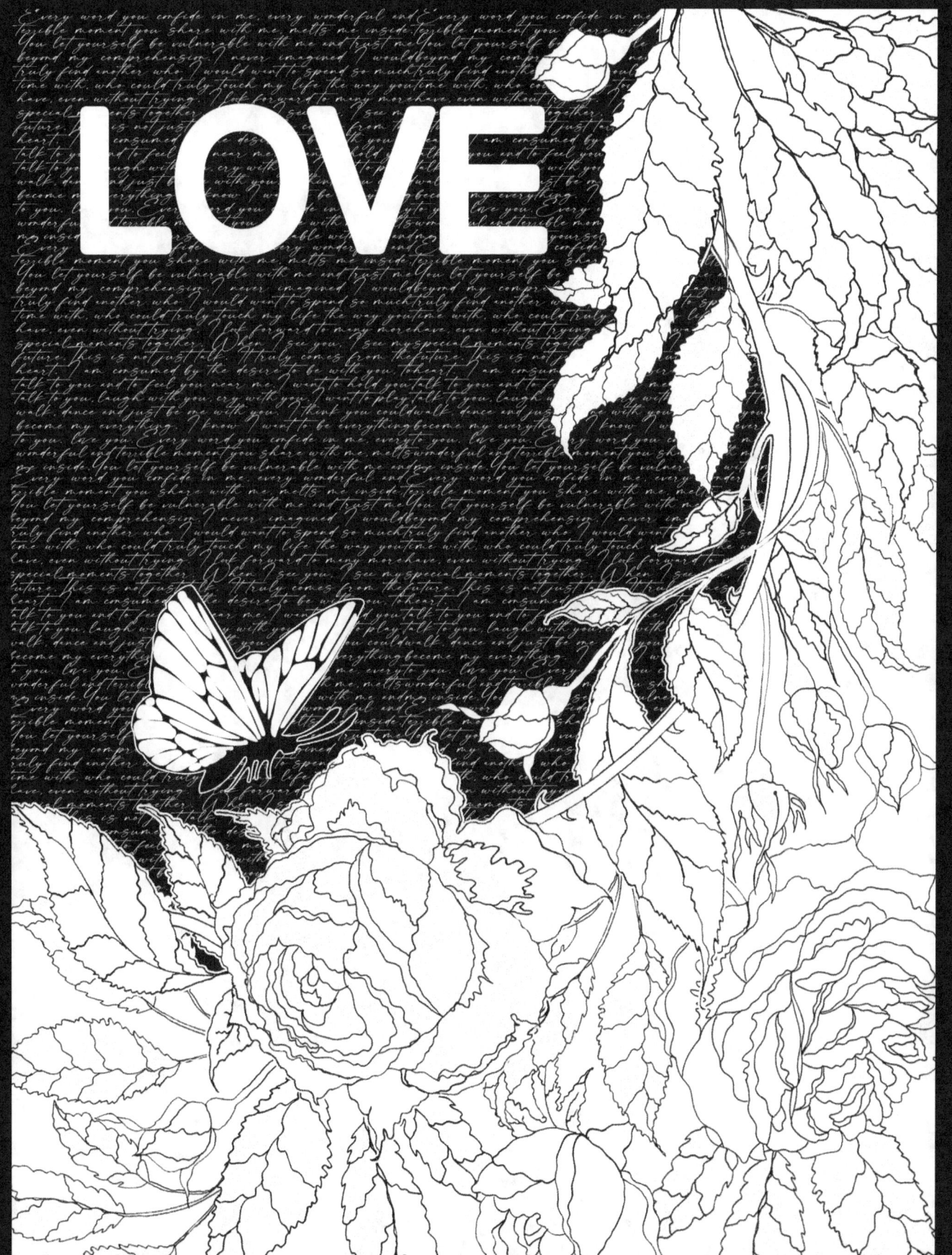

Pears and leaves

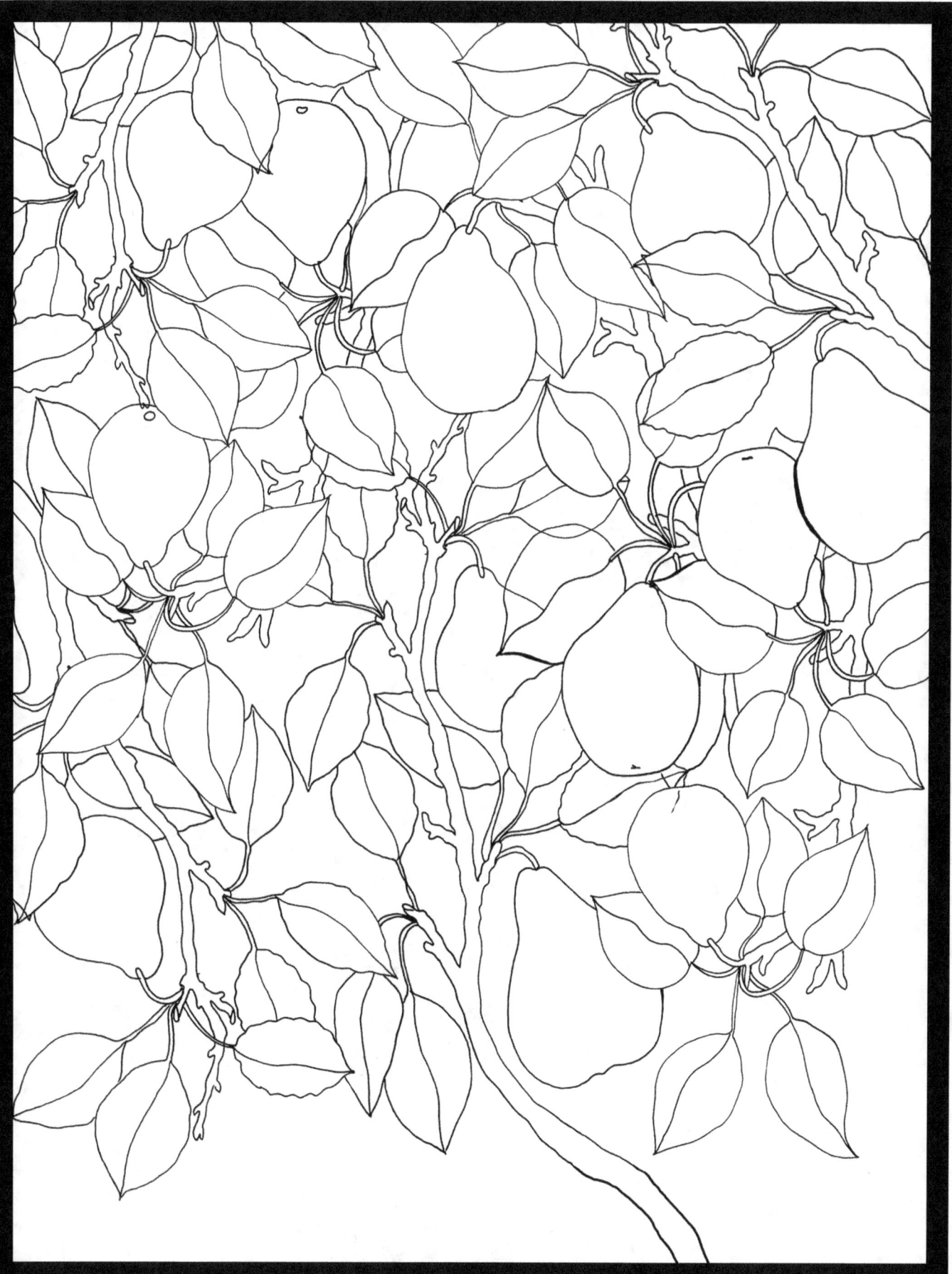

I am thankful

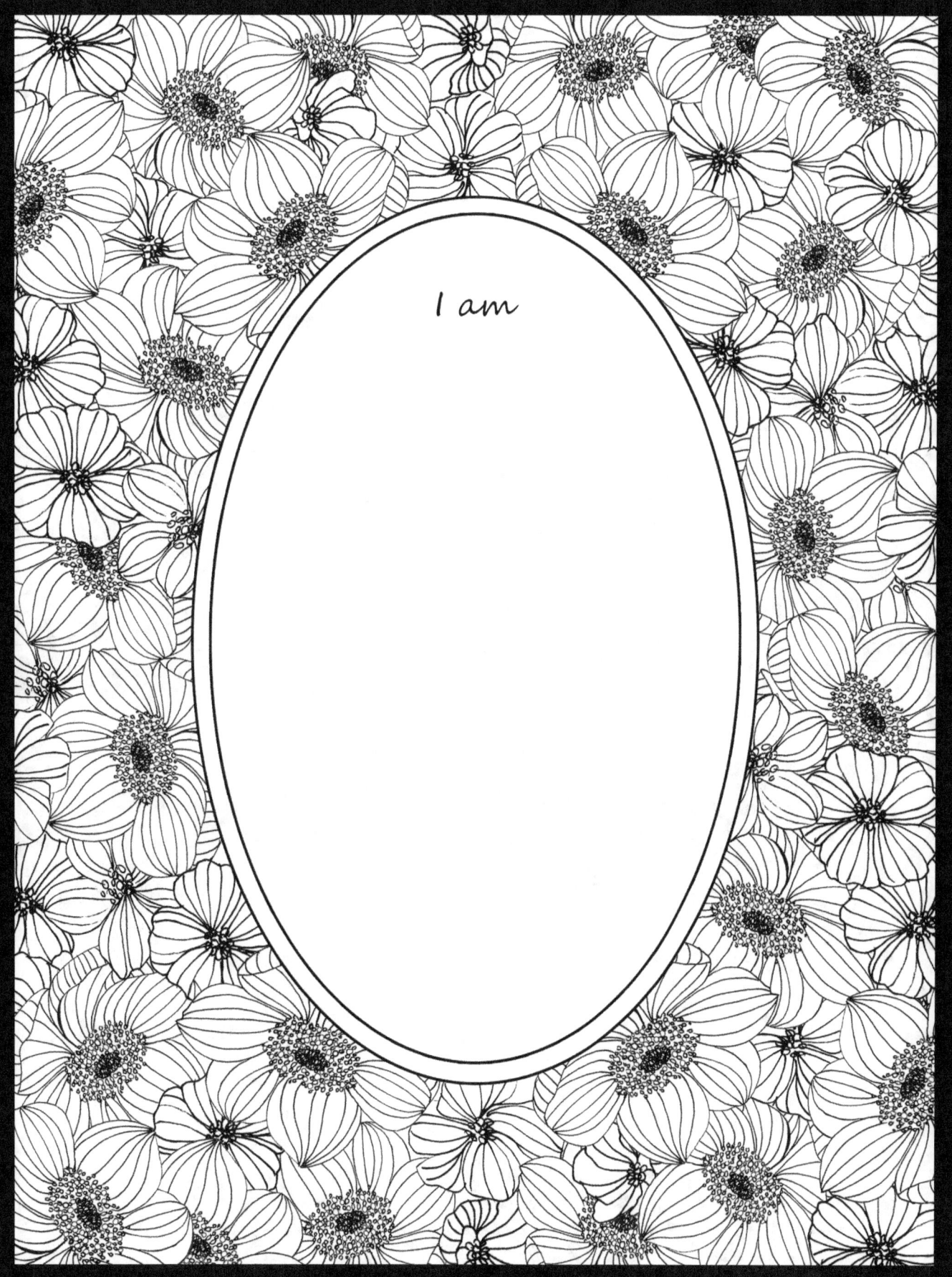

Spring floral frame

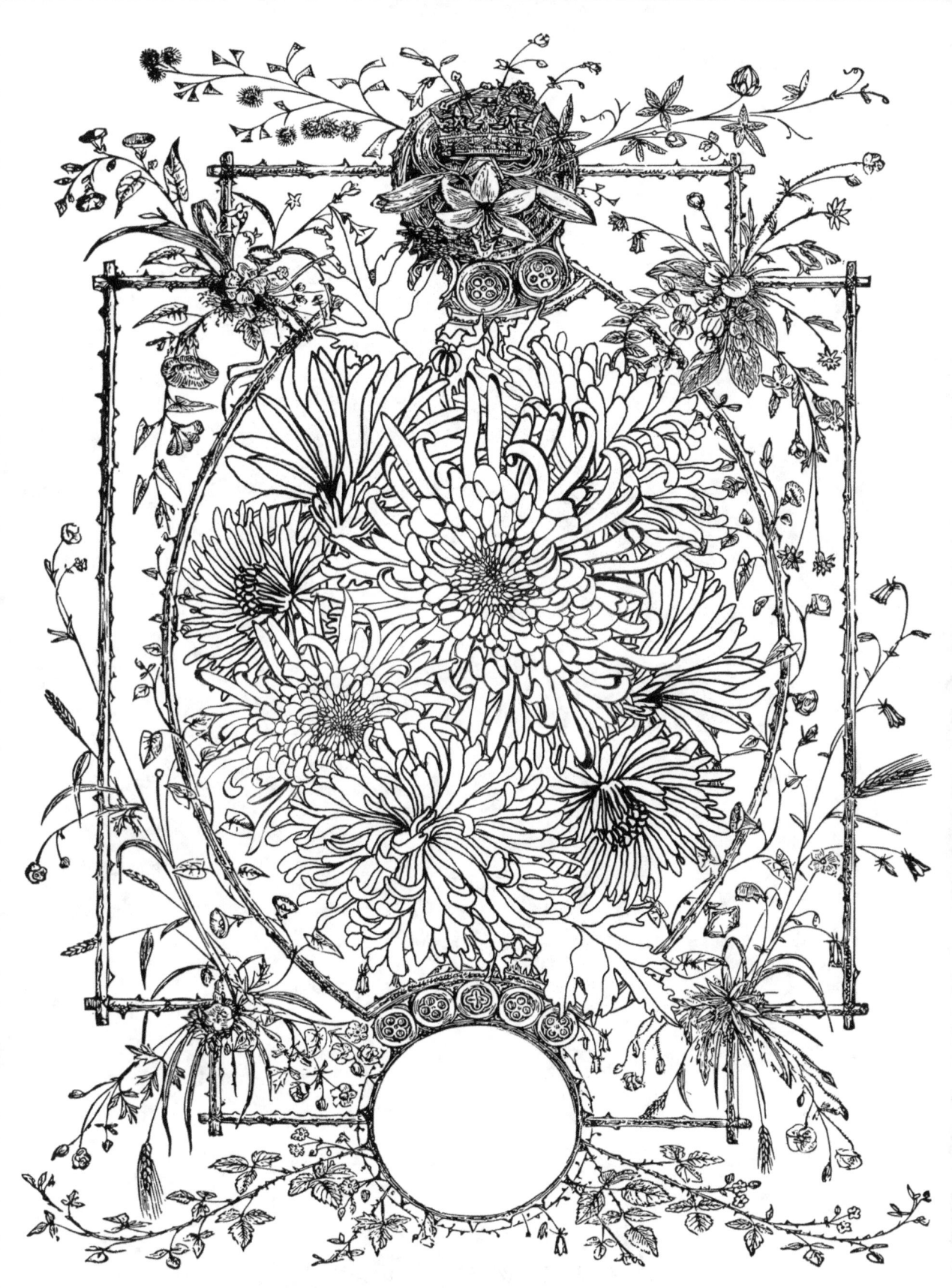

Dancing roses

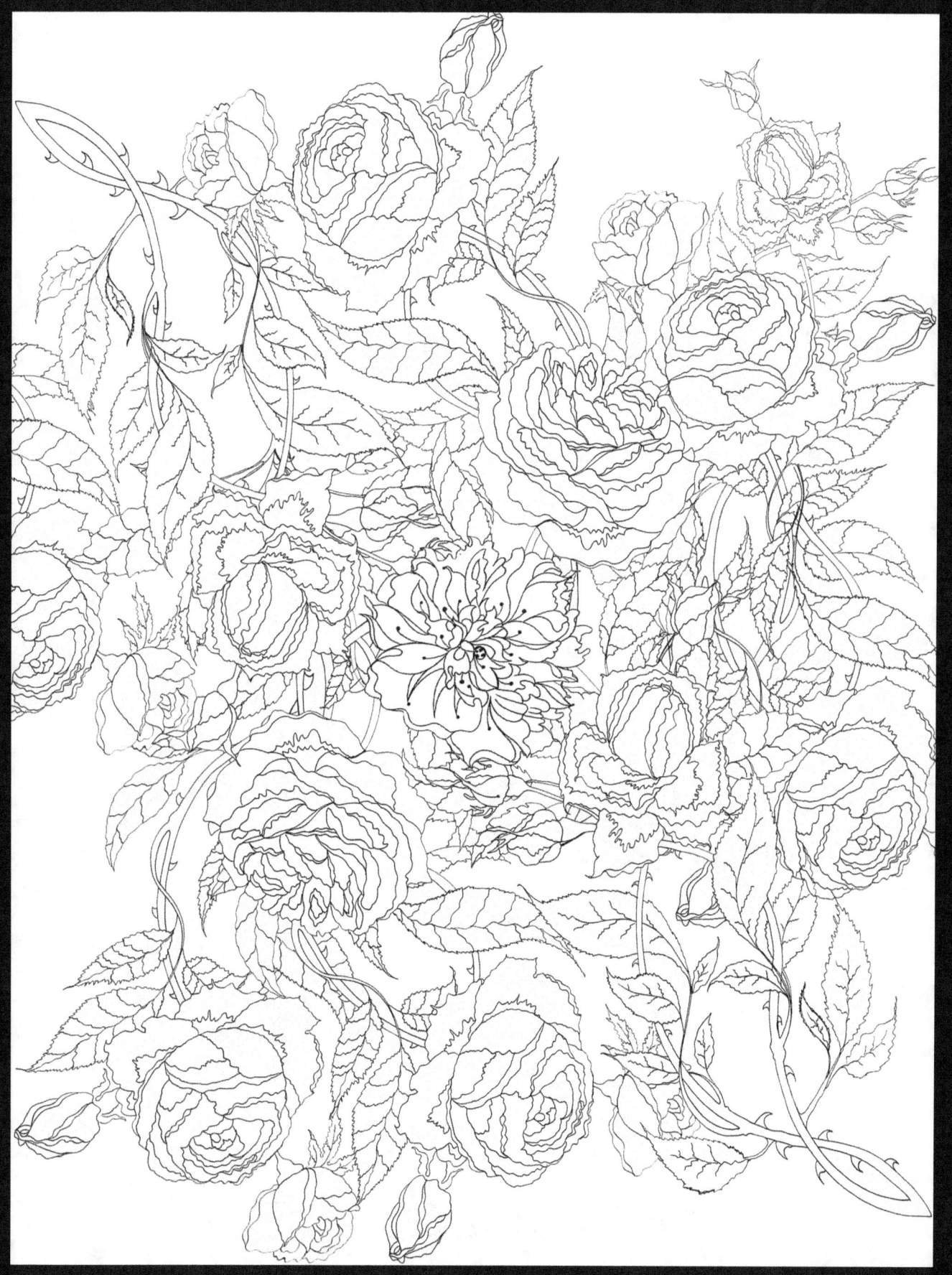

Flowers and hearts

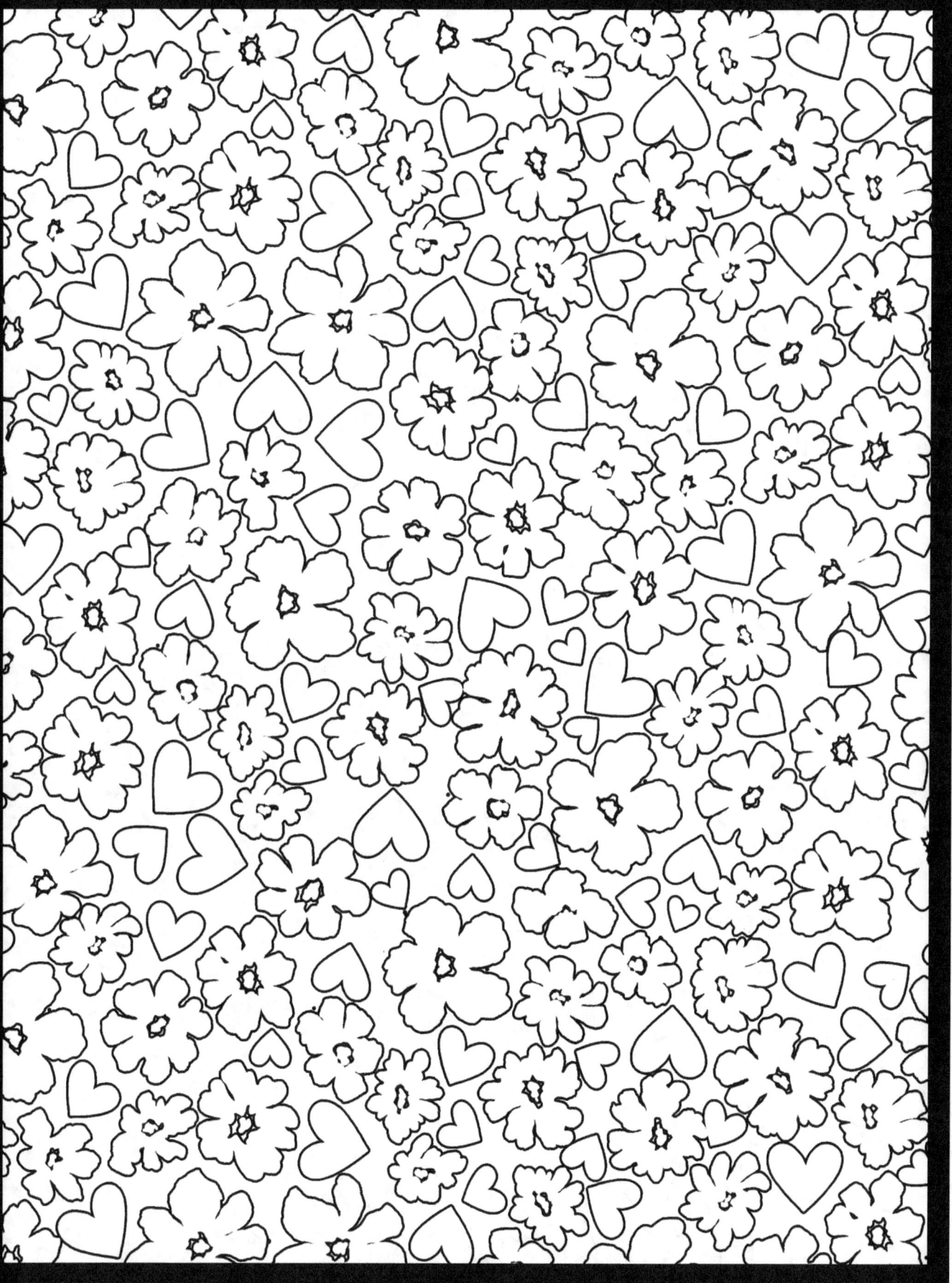

Wiled chrysanthemum

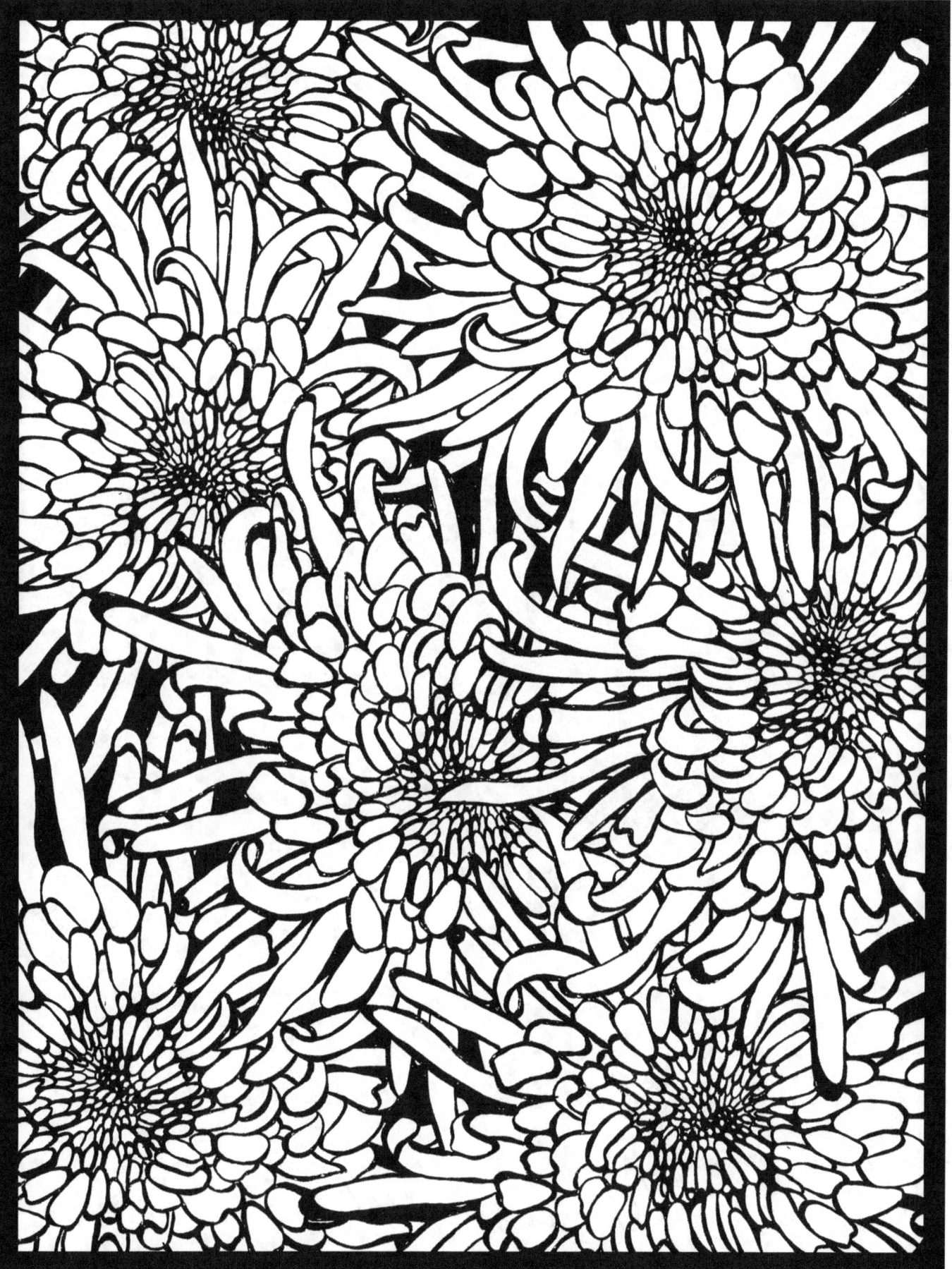

Narcissus flora

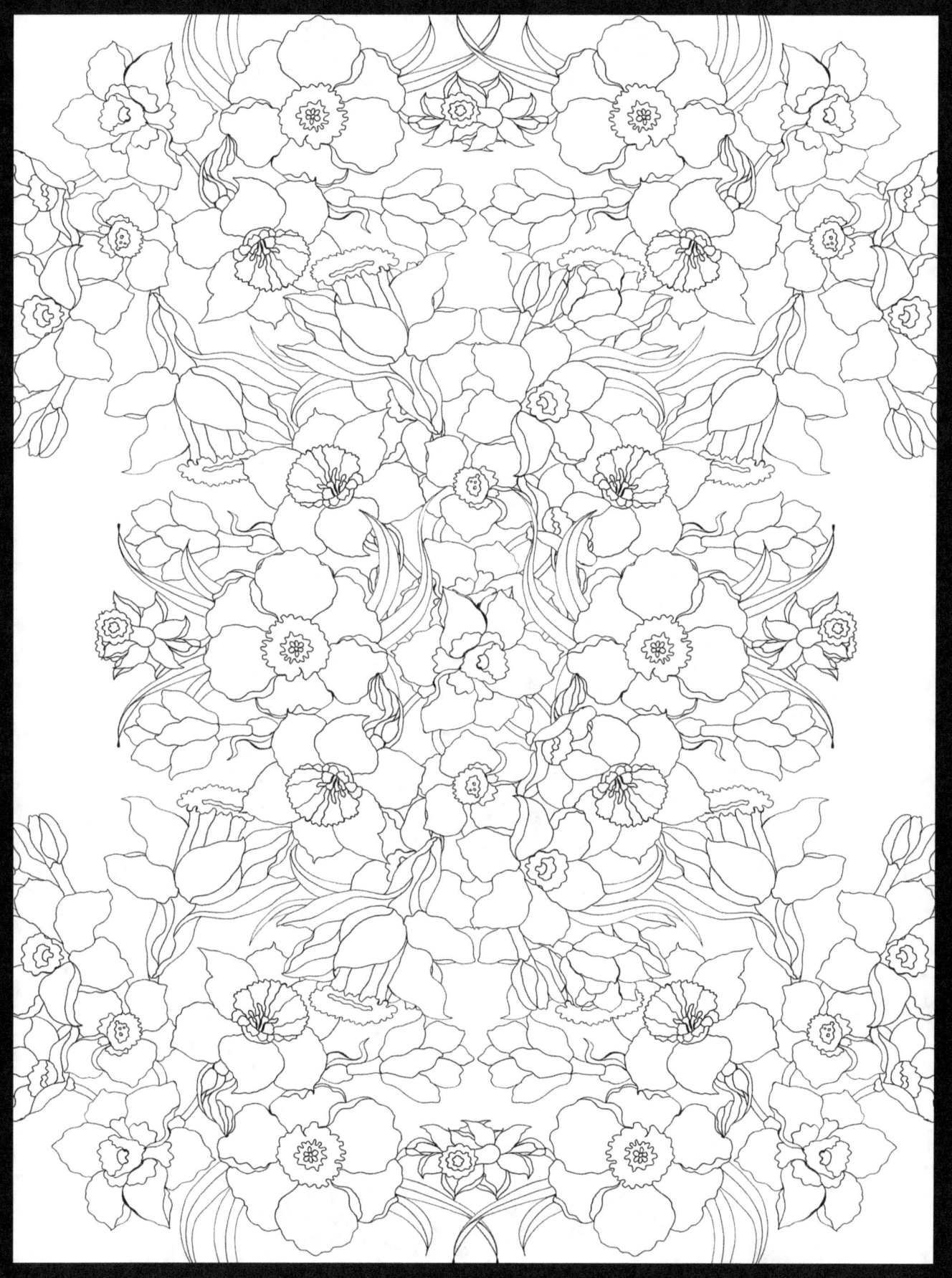

Ourange love

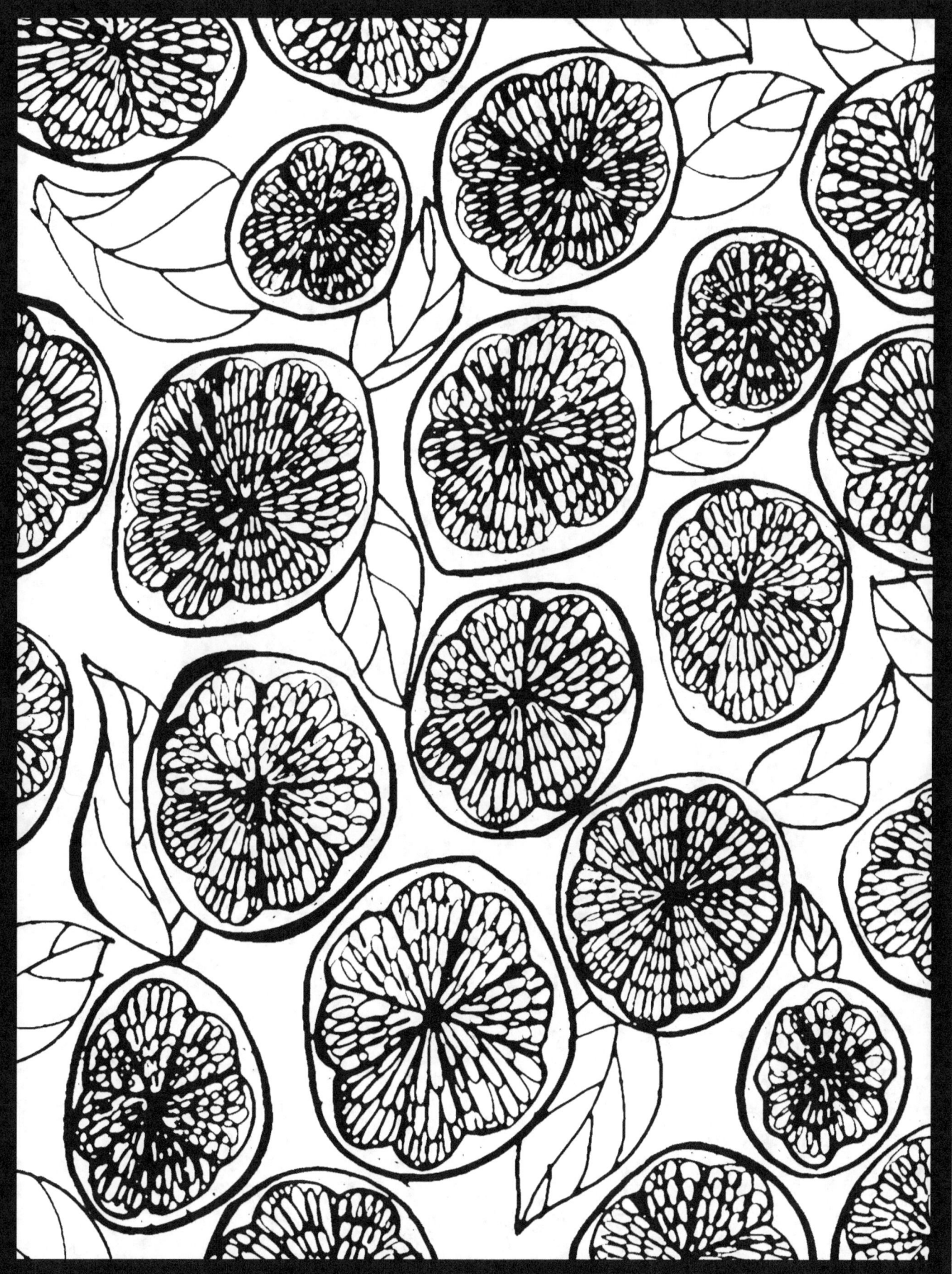

Geometric floral

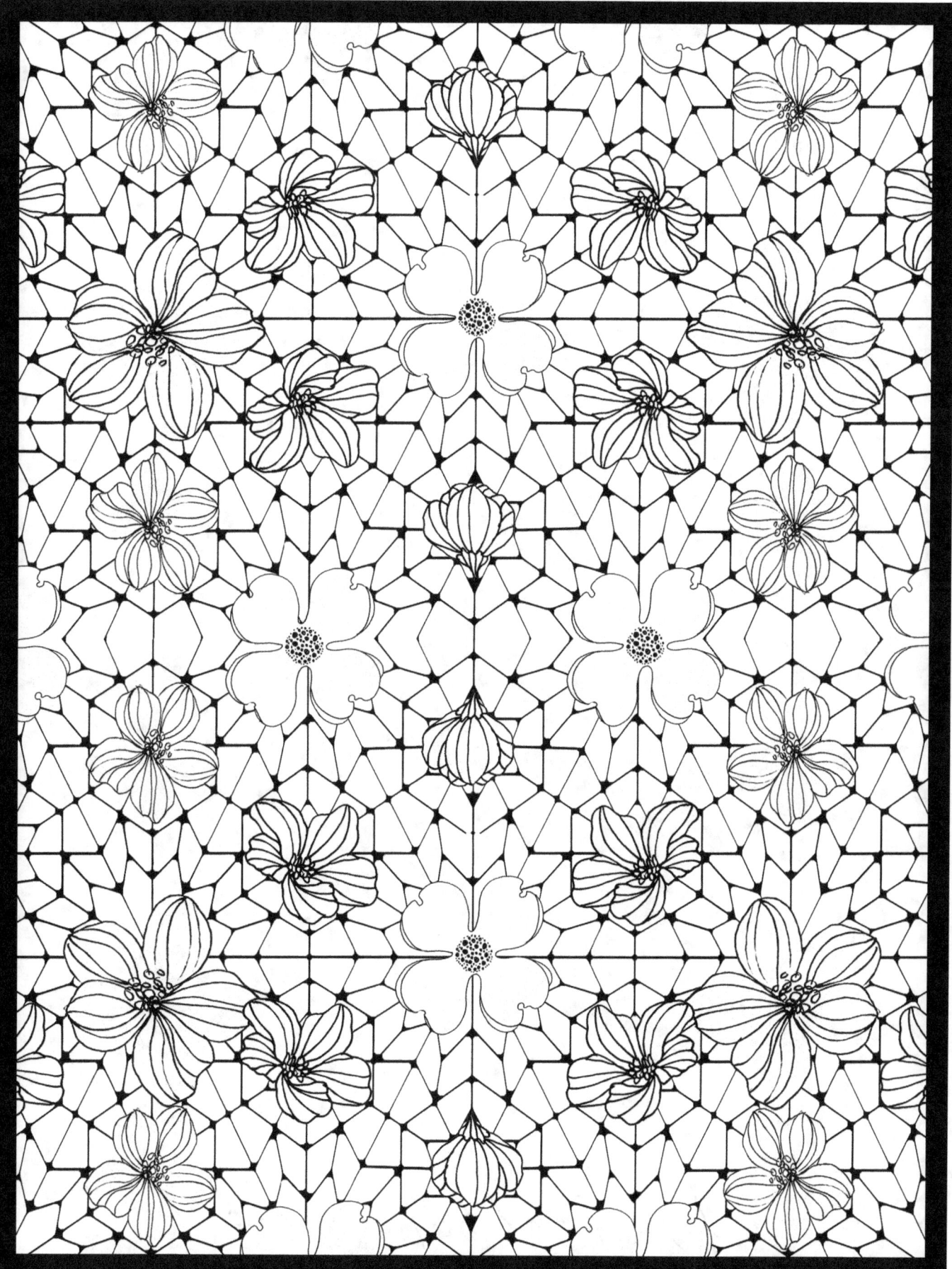

Bird and butterflies

www.ingramcontent.com/pod-product-compliance
Lightning Source LLC
Chambersburg PA
CBHW081700220526
45466CB00009B/2831